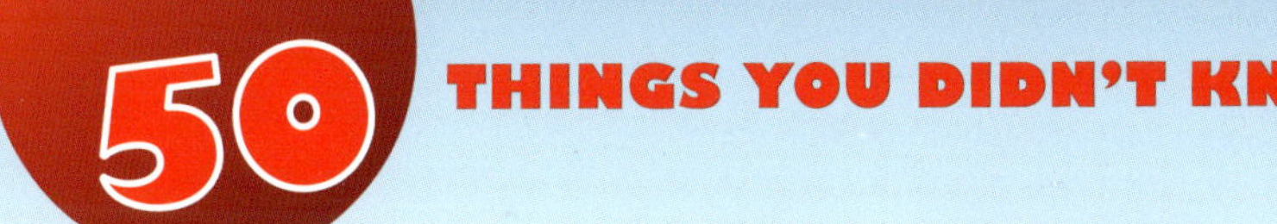

Great Britain

Written and Illustrated
by Sean O'Neill

Egremont, Massachusetts

50 Things You Didn't Know About is produced and published by Red Chair Press:
www.redchairpress.com

FREE lesson guide at www.redchairpress.com/free-activities

Publisher's Cataloging-In-Publication Data

(Provided by Cassidy Cataloging Services, Inc)

Names: O'Neill, Sean, 1968- author, illustrator. | O'Neill, Sean, 1968 50 things you didn't know about (Series)

Title: 50 things you didn't know about Great Britain / written and illustrated by Sean O'Neill.

Other Titles: Great Britain

Description: Egremont, Massachusetts : Red Chair Press, [2024] | Interest age level: 006-009. | Includes bibliographical references and index. | Summary: With 50 Things You Didn't Know About Great Britain young readers will discover the highlights of Great Britain's ancient history, modern traditions and discover unique aspects of food and daily life in Great Britain.--Publisher.

Identifiers: ISBN: 978-1-64371-330-4 (library hardcover) | 978-1-64371-331-1 (softcover) | 978-1-64371-332-8 (ebook) | LCCN: 2023936722

Subjects: LCSH: Great Britain--History--Juvenile literature. | Great Britain--Description and travel-- Juvenile literature. | Great Britain--Social life and customs--Juvenile literature. | CYAC: Great Britain--History. | Great Britain--Description and travel. | Great Britain--Social life and customs. | BISAC: JUVENILE NONFICTION / Travel. | JUVENILE NONFICTION / People & Places / Europe.

Classification: LCC: DA27.5 .O54 2024 | DDC: 941--dc23

Printed in the United States of America

0524 1P F24CG

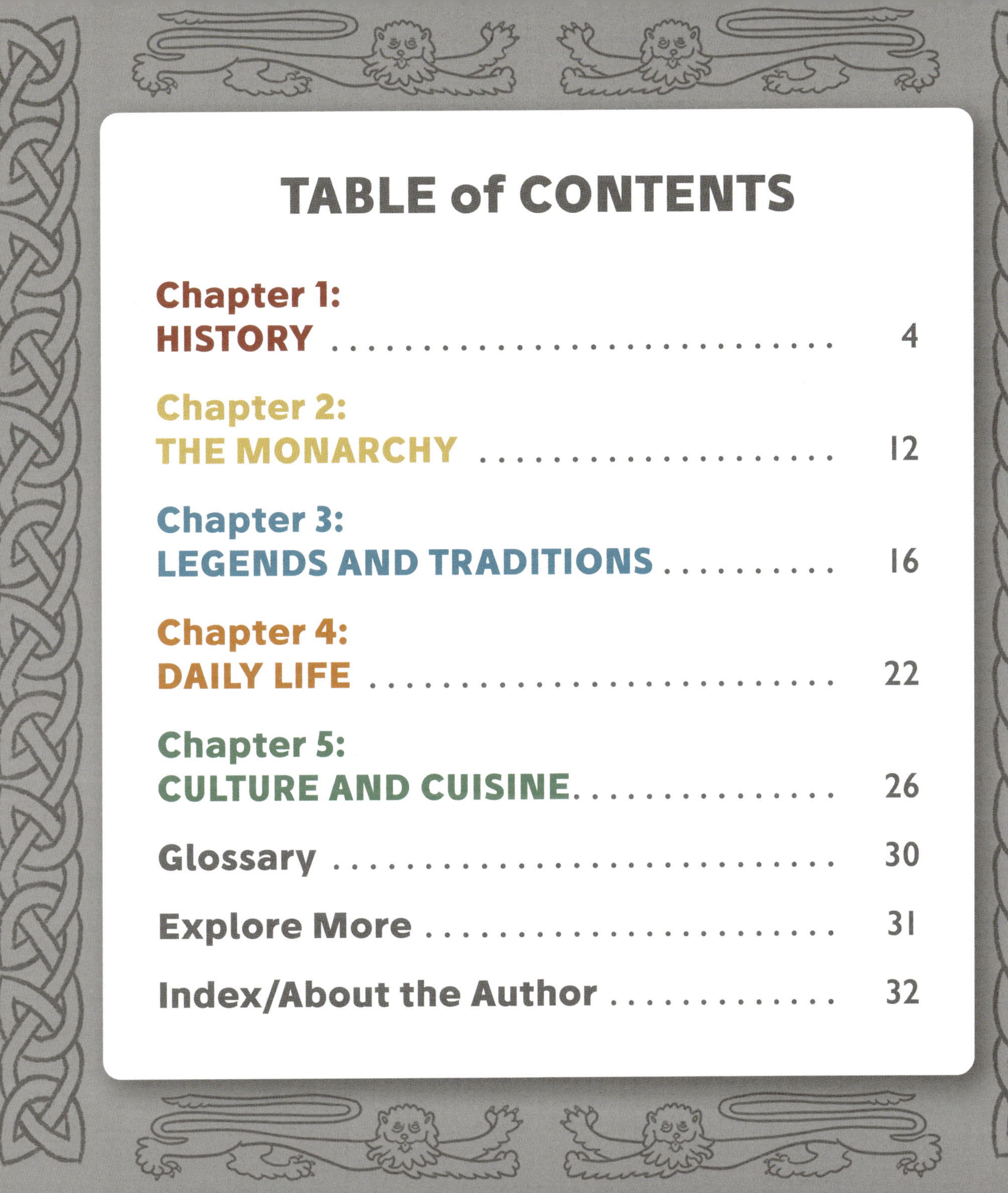

TABLE of CONTENTS

CHAPTER 1

HISTORY

The British Isles were formed 8,500 years ago when melting glaciers created the English Channel, separating the islands from the European continent. Over the centuries, many tribal groups arrived on the island and formed the foundation of British culture. From these prehistoric beginnings, Britain would build an empire that spanned the globe. Today the **United Kingdom*** is a thriving, diverse country with a bustling economy, and a proud cultural tradition that goes back centuries.

*The country's official name is the United Kingdom of Great Britian and Northern Ireland.

1 What is Great Britain, anyway? ***Great Britain*** is actually the name of the island that contains **England**, **Scotland**, and **Wales**. The nation called the **United Kingdom** includes **Great Britian** plus **Northern Ireland**. Got all that?

2 Most of the people we think of as British actually came from somewhere else. First the Celts came from central Europe, then the Romans from Italy, Angles and Saxons from northern Germany, Vikings from Denmark, and, finally, the Normans from France. Today millions of immigrants from around the world call Britain home.

3 Because of the size and shape of the island, no place in Britain is more than 78 miles from the ocean. No wonder they like fish and chips so much.

4 One of the enduring mysteries of British history is Stonehenge—the ancient rock formation believed to have been built by Celtic settlers. No one knows how this structure was built, but it couldn't have been easy. The largest stones weigh 50 tons!

5 Stonehenge was built about 2,300 B.C.E., making it nearly 4,500 years old—older than the great pyramid of Giza in Egypt.

6 Britain was part of the Roman Empire for about 400 years. The Romans built roads and water systems throughout the island. The island's original name comes from the Romans' term for the territory—***Britannia***.

7 The British natives didn't accept Roman rule easily. A legendary Celtic Queen named Boudicca led an army in revolt, and it took 10,000 Roman soldiers to stop her.

8 After 100 years or so, the Romans grew tired of fighting the locals, so they built a wall in Scotland called Hadrian's Wall to keep the troublesome rebels out.

9 Early Anglo-Saxons worshiped Norse gods, and many of our days of the week are named for them. Tiw's Day (Tuesday), Woden's Day (Wednesday), Friya's Day (Friday), and Thursday, which was named for one god you've probably heard of—Thor's Day.

10 William the Conqueror became the first Norman king of England when his army invaded in 1066. He soon built the famous Tower of London, not to protect him from foreign invaders, but from his own people, who weren't happy with Norman rule.

11 A Welsh prince named Madoc, who sailed west seeking new lands, claimed to have found the American continent in 1169, three hundred years before Columbus.

12 King Richard I the Lion-Hearted was so focused on fighting far-away Crusades that he only spent six months of his entire life in Britain, and never bothered to learn English (he was born in France). That's right; a French person became King of England.

13 Queen Elizabeth I, who reigned in the 16th century (1500s), was so popular that ladies at court tried to copy her appearance, even blacking their teeth with soot to match Elizabeth's decaying teeth.

14 The nation of Great Britain was officially created in 1707, when the Kingdoms of England and Scotland were united and formed a single **parliament**.

15 British history is filled with tales of military drama and adventure, but the British can also lay claim to history's shortest war: The Anglo-Zanzibar War of 1896, which lasted only 38 minutes!

16 Britain's Lady with the Lamp—Florence Nightingale—was an English nurse who traveled to Ukraine to care for wounded British soldiers during the Crimean War (1850s). She earned her nickname from her nighttime rounds through the sick wards.

17 British women were granted the right to vote in 1928, eight years after American women.

18 One of the most famous criminals in history is Jack the Ripper, a murderer who terrorized London in 1888. He's referred to as Jack but nobody knows the killer's name. The grisly crimes were never solved.

CHAPTER 2

THE MONARCHY

There are still many active monarchies in the world, but none has captured the world's imagination quite like the British crown. From ancient tales of Camelot and the Knights of the Round Table to the drama surrounding Harry and Meghan, we can't seem to get enough of British royalty. Some of these surprising facts may help explain our fascination.

19 Traditionally, the British King or Queen had considerable power. But there were rules. For example, to this day the Monarch can't set foot in the House of Commons in British Parliament. It's not surprising. The last king who did it was Charles I in the 17th century, and he wound up getting his head cut off!

20 Speaking of beheading… King Henry VIII married six times and beheaded *two* of his wives all to try to have a male heir. But it was all for nothing; Henry died without a son to take over the throne, the daughter from his second wife became Queen Elizabeth I.

21 The late-Queen Elizabeth II became Britain's longest reigning monarch in 2022 after 70 years on the throne. Compare that to Lady Jane Grey, who in 1554 sat on the throne for only nine days. After that she was—you guessed it! —beheaded!

22 King James II was so unpopular that in 1688 members of his court invited his daughter Mary and her husband William to invade England from Scotland and overthrow him.

23 The Royal Family has several official residences. One of them, Windsor Castle, is the oldest inhabited castle in the world.

24 The primary Royal residence, Buckingham Palace, has 775 rooms, including 78 bathrooms!

25 According to tradition, the British Monarch owns all of the swans in Britain. I don't know who has to feed them.

26 The famous black fur hats worn by Buckingham Palace guards are made from bearskin, and can weigh up to nine pounds.

27 The King's Royal Guards have the nickname "Beefeaters," because in the 14th Century they began a tradition of eating roast beef every Sunday.

CHAPTER 3

LEGENDS AND TRADITIONS

Kings! Queens! Knights! Wizards! Monsters! The history and folklore of Great Britain is filled with so many familiar characters and legends that it can sometimes be hard to separate fact from fiction. Some of the real traditions in British culture can be harder to believe than the legends of swords and sorcery.

28 King Arthur is a legendary figure, but there may be some truth to the story. An ancient text called *The History of the Kings of Britain* tells of a King Arthur who reigned from the end of Roman rule until the year 542, 500 years before William the Conqueror.

29 Another English legend, the swashbuckling hero Robin Hood, is likely based on a real person—Robyn Hood—who was a member of the king's court in 1324.

30 Every 5th of November, British people celebrate Guy Fawkes Day. Although the holiday is named for him, he's no hero. In 1605 Fawkes attempted to blow up Parliament with barrels of gunpowder. His plan was thwarted, and the date is oddly celebrated with fireworks and bonfires.

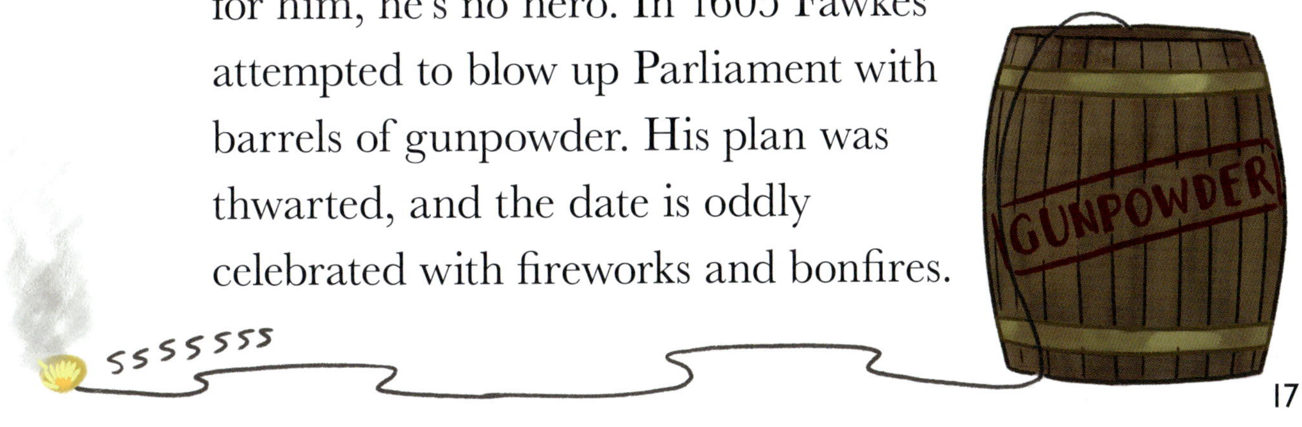

GUNPOWDER

SSSSSSS

31 The British really do have some unusual traditions. In the town of Gloucestershire, one Sunday night a year, basketfuls of bread and cheese are thrown from atop the castle walls. Citizens try to grab as many pieces as they can.

32 If you're into flying cheese, be sure to check out the Spring Cheese Rolling competition. Wheels of cheese are rolled down a hill and players try to be the first to grab them. But be careful! It's not uncommon for participants to suffer sprained ankles or broken limbs.

33 The British do love games and sports. Great Britain is the birthplace of golf, tennis, soccer, rugby, and cricket. Golf was created in Scotland, although the game was banned briefly in 1457 because the King wanted men to take up archery instead.

34 One of the most popular sports in Britain is cricket. The game is famously complicated, and matches can last up to five days. There's also some pretty odd terminology in the rules.

35 Traditionally, 6 black ravens live in the famous Tower of London. King Charles II decreed in the 1600s that if any of them flew away, the kingdom would fall. To prevent this, the birds' wings are clipped (humanely, of course).

36 One of Scotland's most famous residents is Nessie, also known as the Loch Ness Monster. In 1962 a government commission was formed to investigate sightings of the creature, but as yet has produced no real evidence.

37 According to British law, all horses (and ponies) must have a British passport.

38 The famous Union Jack flag of Great Britain is a combination of the traditional flags of England, Scotland, and North Ireland. Wales has a flag, too, but it seems they didn't have room for the big, red dragon.

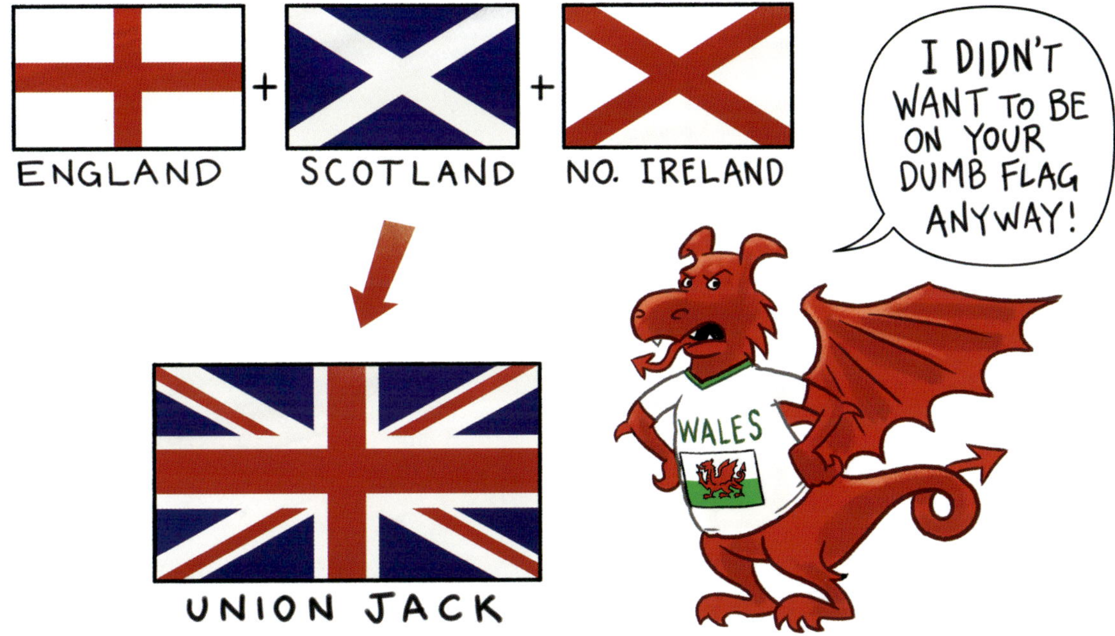

CHAPTER 4

DAILY LIFE

Despite the **medieval** castles and Roman **aqueducts**, today's Great Britain is a modern diverse nation that is a center of international trade and a destination for millions of tourists and immigrants. On the surface, British life may seem familiar, but on closer examination you may find some of these facts to be a little unusual.

39 The city of London was the largest (most populous) city on Earth from about 1830 until 1925, with a population of over 7 million.

40 English is obviously the official language in Britain, but their version may sound a little different to American ears. An apartment is a "flat," baby diapers are "nappies," and you ride up and down in a "lift" (not an elevator).

41 Most visitors to London will tell you that they saw Big Ben. But *did* they? Big Ben is actually not the famous clock tower (that's called Elizabeth Tower), but the large bell inside it that chimes every hour.

42 Beneath London's King's Cross train station there are huge underground wells for storing ice. There was no refrigeration in Victorian times, so these wells stored ice year-round for serving cold drinks and ice cream.

43 The British invented the postage stamp. The first adhesive stamp was introduced in 1840 and had a picture of Queen Victoria on it.

44 The longest known place name in Europe is the Welsh town of—ready for this? —Llanfairpwllgwyngyllgogerychwyrndrob-wllllllandysiliogogogoch. That's a mouthful!

45 Britain is filled with unusually-named towns and streets, including Badger's Mound, Sandy Bottom, and WhamBottom Lane.

CHAPTER 5

CULTURE AND CUISINE

What could be more British than a cuppa, or cup of tea, a Shakespeare **sonnet**, and a mincemeat pie? British culture has given us many of our favorite characters, stories, and even a few new words. And even if jellied eels doesn't sound like your "cup of tea," maybe some of these facts will whet your appetite.

46 One of the most famous Brits in history is the great playwright William Shakespeare. Shakespeare added several new words to the English language in his plays and sonnets, including *gossip, zany, and alligator.*

47 Shakespeare died in 1616, and left this warning on his grave:

> *Blest be the man that spares these stones*
> *And curst be the man that moves my bones.*

So far, the curse has worked. His grave is exactly where he left it in Stratford-upon-Avon.

48 There are many interesting (and unusual) British foods, but when Brits recently voted for a national dish, they chose one from India—the curry dish Chicken Tikka Masala.

49 Speaking of unusual, next time you visit Great Britain, be sure to try some jellied eels, turkey twizzlers, bubble and squeak, flies graveyard, and mushy peas.

50 The world's most famous secret agent, James Bond, was created by English writer Ian Fleming. Bond's legendary code name came from a bus route near Fleming's home—the 007 bus route, from Canterbury to Kent.

Glossary

aqueducts: structures usually made of stone built to carry water across valleys.

Medieval: from the Middle Ages, 5th to 15th Centuries.

parliament: In England Parliament is made of 2 groups: the House of Commons and the House of Lords.

sonnet: The verses of a Shakespearean sonnet are divided into three parts with four lines each, followed by one rhyming couplet, or rhyming verse with two lines.

Learn More about Great Britian

Brassey, Richard and Stewart Ross. *The Story of Scotland*. Orion Children's Books, 1999.

Forrester, Kate. *Celtic Tales: Fairy Tales and Stories of Enchantment from Ireland, Scotland, Brittany, and Wales.* Chronicle Books, 2016.

Scott, Janine and Peter Rees. *Great Britian: Everything You Ever Wanted to Know*. Lonely Planet Publications and Weldon Owen Ltd, 2012.

Stover, Logan. *Let's Learn About England.* Kid Planet Books, 2021.

Stover, Logan. *Let's Learn About Scotland.* Kid Planet Books, 2021.

Williams, Imogene Russell. *The Big Book of the U.K. Facts, Folklore and Fascinations.* Ladybird Books, 2019.

Index

About the Author/Illustrator

Sean O'Neill is an illustrator and writer living in Chicago. He is the creator of *50 Things You Didn't Know* and the *Rocket Robinson* series of graphic novels. Sean loves history, trivia, and drawing cartoons, so this project is pretty much a dream assignment, and it comes with bubble and squeak.